Love Lotus

A Collection of Poems

Shruti Diwan

India | USA | UK

Made with ❤ on the BookLeaf Publishing Platform

www.bookleafpub.in

www.bookleafpub.com

Dedication

Dedicated to YOU.

Whether you are beginning your healing journey or deep within it, may these words bring you comfort, insight, and inspiration.

Preface

Welcome to *Love Lotus*, a collection of poems born from my heart. Writing these poems has been a way for me to share my journey with you, and I hope they resonate with the part of you that is seeking healing, peace, and growth.

In these pages, you'll find reflections on spirituality, awakening, love, and nature. Each poem is a step along the path I've traversed, and I invite you to experience it with me.

Acknowledgements

A huge thank you to my dear husband Santosh, for being my unwavering supporter and for always believing in me.

Your constant encouragement in all my endeavours has given me the strength to pursue my passions and bring *Love Lotus* to life. I am forever grateful for your love and patience.

Dance of the Divine

In the movie of life, we pick roles to portray.

We play heroes and villains.

We play victors and victims.

We play givers and takers.

Drop the masks.

Behind the scenes, we are all one.

Deeply connected.

Joyfully experiencing the dance of the Divine.

Art of Allowing

Affirming
Journaling
Praying
Vision boarding
Struggling
Until my awakening...
Then it was about allowing.
Allowing every moment to be.
Allowing every person to be.
Allowing every situation to be.
Allowing.

Longing for Home

Not the one with the pretty drapes and a cosy corner full
of books.
Not the one that's filled with the aroma of freshly
brewed coffee and a comfy bed.
Not the one with the knick-knacks and cuddly pets.

The one that sets my soul on fire.
The one that awakens me.
The one that's an enlightening dark night.

Nameless

Oft compelled to name each connection encountered on
life's journey...
Once in a blue moon a bond blooms beyond names...
Unconditional.
Undying.
Unbreakable.

Alchemy

Slogging through the Redwood forest
Towering trees of expectations, enmeshment, emptiness
Sensing herself small
Trudging an uncharted path
Slowly but surely
Transmuting the anguish, anxiety, agitation
Sunlight beaming through the tallest trees...

Southern Lights

Leaning on the wall of the dam
Waiting impatiently for the sky to put up a glam

The lights didn't show
Disappointing, I know

Driving back home, a wave of strangeness swept over me
Feeling profoundly connected to every mountain, sea, and tree

A sensation I couldn't shake
Sleep is a stranger, now that I'm finally awake

Fear

Even joy's light casts mighty shadows of fear.
Fear of being unconditionally loved.
Fear of being seen.
Fear of being heard.
Fear of being held.
Fear of the truth.
Fear of shining.
Fear.
Strangely primal.
Rarely rational.
Definitely transmutable.

Redefining Success

Conned into believing that success is...

Constant busyness

Competition

C-suite position

Chauffeur driven C-class

Chasing cash

Conscious enough to redefine success as...

Contentment

Creative exploration

Community connection

Courage

Confidence

Creativity

Overflowing is the fountain of creativity
The more you use it
The more it flows
Your artistry shines and glows

The Phoenix

The battle of picking yourself up is winnable
Because...
You are worthy
You are whole
You are a WARRIOR

Love Lotus

Sprouting deep in the murky waters of
pain and patriarchy

Growing strong in a
hot and hostile environment

Rising unscathed above the surface of
suppression and solitude

Blooming resiliently into a
love lotus

Ephemeral Journey

In a world of constant connectedness
You endure more and more loneliness

Why are you really here?
No, tell me my dear...

Did you come to pay bills and die?
Tell yourself another lie?

Did you take up roles they pushily ask?
Did you daringly drop your mask?

Did you attempt to find your true nature?
And choose love at every juncture?

Whether insignificant or incredible
This journey is eerily ephemeral...

The Guest

Days were passing by
Enjoying the charming irrelevancies of life
One chilly morning
I heard a thunderous knock
The kind that shatters illusions
I rushed to open the door
There she stood
Elegantly ecstatic
Blood red lips
Raven black cloak
The stranger I knew I'd meet
I was ready to shed the old
Mother Death's cold yet compassionate embrace
Liberated me with grace

Grief

The childhood you never had
The one-sided friendship that ended
The trauma you endured
The unmet needs
The sacrifices you chose to make
The home you lost
The dreams you relinquished

Grieve...
When you grieve, you accept.
Deep acceptance paves the path to healing.

Wholeness

The world will constantly pressure you
into believing that
your existence has
no purpose
if you don't bear a child

In case you needed a reminder...
Your body
Your life
Your rules

Inner Child

My dear inner child...
I'm sorry I abandoned you for so long

You are not a burden
You are not stupid

You are loved
You are beautiful

You deserve to be seen and heard
You deserve to be cherished

Your feelings matter
Your voice matters

You are worthy of everything and then some more!
Don't let anyone tell you otherwise

Illusion

Time keeps weaving an illusory yarn

Tell your person how much you love them
Write that book you always wanted to publish
Take the trip you've been putting off
Work on your passion project
Call your long-lost friend

Live now
Love now
Be happy now

The Mirror

When you're not searching for them
They show up in your life
The person who has the other end
Of the red string of fate tied to their finger
Life's circumstances and choices have led to
THIS moment
Gazing into their eyes feels like
Looking into the mirror of eternity
Life never seems the same ever again

Eternal Love

I'll say I love you
Every moment
Like a silent prayer
Until my last breath

Love by Any Other Name

Love

Pyar

Liebe

Amore

Name it what you will...

KNOW that it is the beauty and truth of Your existence!

A Glimpse of Paradise

God is an artist they say
Indeed, She is! One of the finest artists
Her canvas has a different painting every day
She created the earth in Her own right
Probably to give us a glimpse of paradise
A brilliant flash of colours in a serene sunset or dark
clouds of a rusty rainy day
The lush green forests or the shimmering blue waters
The pure white snow or the golden sand
The strikingly beautiful flowers or the gigantic trees
The dazzling rainbow or the scintillating dew drops on
grass
The alluring & ever mystical moon
Every shade & tint used with panache
But above all She created the sun
The light of which energises every soul
The sun, which gives tremendous hope by rising every
day & illuminating the world engulfed in darkness
Giving a message to all, that the pitch black night is
ALWAYS defeated by light!